GOLD MINDS

To Jesse and Kendra – My future Gold Minds

………, to Emelia De Lawrence - My Wife

…… and to Daniel, Shirley, my brother and sisters, for always being there for me

GOLD MINDS

Obeng De Lawrence

[British education in Retrospect]
A Case for POSSIBLE LINKS BETWEEN SYSTEMS OF EDUCATION AND NATIONAL DEVELOPMENT

© Obeng De Lawrence 2009

First Published in 2009

All rights reserved. No part of this publication may be reproduced or transmitted in any form or by any means, electronic or mechanical, including photocopying, recording, or any information storage or retrieval system, without prior permission in writing from the publishers.

www.piqxel.com | enquiries@piqxel.com

ISBN: 978-0-9561593-0-4

Printed and bounded by Lulu

Forward

Two decades of working in the field of education in the UK has taught me some great lessons, especially those that contrast sharply with my own experience in my homeland of Africa.
In Africa, we were told that our education followed the British system. However, in the UK, my experience has been almost the opposite.

To start with, I came across a Western education that was and still is in the process of defining itself. Indeed, as I write now, education in Britain is currently undergoing several changes and is set to do so for the foreseeable future. These may be due to several factors that may contribute to the need to modify or improve educational standards.

This book paints a picture of a golden box, with people inside and outside. Those inside appear to want to help those struggling on the outside.
Those outside are desperate, reaching out to grab whatever is on offer from inside the box with the hope of finding a solution to their problems.

But both those inside and outside the box struggle with the problem of how to turn what is on offer into gold for those who had it before and have lost most of it to those inside. Ironically those outside the box need to recover or discover their gold desperately for their own recovery and survival.

In this book, I share my thoughts as someone who once observed the box from the outside but now struggles from inside to reach out to those both within and outside the box. Those within the box are the architects of and policy makers for British education as well as its stakeholders within the UK. Those outside are all those who subscribe to British education, from the developing and Third Worlds wherever they may be.

Abstract

In this book I have made an attempt to uncover the secret behind Great Britain's ability to turn their land once filled with coal to a land full of gold. Most of the discussion is centred on key factors and systems of education as well as the kind of people that might have contributed to this success,

In doing so, questions are asked as to why the success and wealth of Great Britain is not having the desired impact throughout the empire.

For this reason I have tried to explore with the reader what can be done for the rest of the world to benefit from British or Western education, whatever that may be.

Obeng De Lawrence
www.itclondon.org.uk

Contents

Acknowledgements ix
Introduction xi

Chapter 1	What is Education?	03
Chapter 2	Like Them, system of education	17
Chapter 3	Beyond Us, system of education	23
Chapter 4	British Education?	31
Chapter 5	Defining British education	37
Chapter 6	History of thinking skills development and the Beginnings of Beyond Us, Education	43
Chapter 7	Thinking skills in the UK: More examples of Beyond Us, education	49
Chapter 8	Evidence-based results and progression in British education	57
Chapter 9	British education – A long and Winding Road!	63
Chapter 10	Nurturing future Minds as Agents of Change.	71
Chapter 11	Beyond the Gold Mind – Education, Learning and Skills Revolution for the Twenty First Century	79

References 83

Acknowledgements

I would like to thank the following people for their support and encouragement while I was writing this book.

Ken Evans
Sylvia Howe
Sharon Knight
Lyndon Jennings
Maureen Austin
Marvis Cudjoe
Omotunde Komolafe
Ivan Corea
Lydia Mireku
Joel Agoro

….. And all the staff at ITC London

Introduction

"Necessity is the mother of invention."

Oh, is it? Perhaps for some of us, - but possibly not for all of us.

Abraham Maslow describes human beings as need-driven organisms in his hierarchy of needs.

> **Abraham Maslow** - *a leading educational psychologist developed the Hierarchy of Needs model in 1940-50's USA, that has still remained a significant tool for understanding human motivation, management training, and personal development.. Maslow's ideas surrounding the ' Hierarchy of Needs', creates a platform concerning the responsibility of employers to provide a workplace environment that encourages and enables employees to fulfil their own unique potential (self-actualization). In a nut-shell, society is need driven, and needs will drive us in search for solutions.*

All well and good as far as it goes, but it falls short of explaining apparent differences in communities' abilities to respond to need in a positive way. Necessity has led to some of the greatest lessons and inventions of history in the West, but puzzlingly it has provided few if any lessons for progress in most parts of the world.

In effect, whereas one society is capable of effectively responding to need through invention and creativity, others fall short of responding positively to need, through lack of motivation, means, skill, and creativity. Given that both these groups have their human capacity and fair share

INTRODUCTION

of natural resources, one would expect that these should lead to similar outcomes. The fact that this is not the case has remained a mystery, but not any longer.

Our journey starts and ends in Great Britain – a nation that has managed to create a sustainable empire and wealth from almost nothing except their human capacity and a few natural resources. Its greatest asset has been its people, who explored the world for centuries. Despite starting with few natural resources such as coal, they have managed to prove to the world that intelligent, active and patriotic citizenship is what is needed most, to bring about progress and make a nation 'great'.

By great, I mean whatever it is that attracts people to their colonial master and emperor 'Britain'.

I have discovered in retrospect that some citizens focused on nurturing talents capable of turning a land with coal into a land of gold thereby creating opportunities for their empire and other citizens. In a sense, they had discovered how to make the most of what they had, as well as add to it.

Not only this, they knew what was needed to achieve their end. They needed 'Gold Minds' and there were those who believed in and were committed to growing and nurturing these for future prosperity. Among them are people who experimented with knowledge and expedition, exploring the world and risking their lives in search of 'golden opportunities'. In addition there were others who pursued and made the most of the resources they had at their homeland of the British Isles.

Most of these explorers got what they were looking for and with this have succeeded somehow in creating a sustainable empire that remains active in people's minds throughout the world. Apparently, as a result, every nation on earth today wants a slice of Great Britain, such that demand for things 'British' exceeds supply in almost every sphere including education, language, culture, brand, and taste.

How did Great Britain achieve this and what lessons are there for those that would like to subscribe to this kind of wisdom?

It is generally believed that this kind of development is not unique to Britain but common with their European and Western nations such as France, Germany and the USA, and somehow intrinsic in the systems of education operated in these countries. They too have managed to explore the world in the past for green pastures that were geared towards the benefit of their citizens.

If this is the case then we need to find answers as to why similar results are not achieved in poor nations which spend significant proportions of their gross domestic product on emulating British or Western education.

In this book, I highlight the contrast between two systems and look at the factors including education and culture that need reviewing, in order to ensure recovery or enhance progress within poor countries.

As part of the project, I look critically at the differences between educational strategies in the West and those delivered within schools in the Third World.

Let us hope that this book provides not only food for thought, but also motivation for action, to those wanting to incorporate elements of British education that will contribute towards developing a nation.

This should, I hope, include governments, policy makers, relevant institutions, educators, school managers, teachers, parents, students and learners.

What is Education?

01

Webster defines education as the process of educating or teaching. Educate is further defined as "to develop the knowledge, skill, or character of..."

Unfortunately, definitions like these offer little unless there are attempts to identify or address what education is for or why societies or individuals seek to educate themselves or others.
In my experience there is no single definition of education other than what one or the other society thinks it is or would like it to be.

This has led me to categorise it as three main systems that are being operated across the world. These may be classified as:
- Like Us
- Like Them
- Beyond Us

And may be described as follows:

Like Us system of education
This system of education aims at schooling learners to be what society is today. The teacher or educator believes that society has reached a stage where it knows everything. Learners are expected to take instructions from their teachers and reproduce them just as they were told. Educators in this category define education as a way of imparting knowledge.

```
        LIKE US                    LIKE THEM
           ↑                           ↑
           │                           │
           └──────┐           ┌────────┘
                  │           │
            ┌─────────────────────┐
            │ EDUCATIONAL SYSTEMS │
            │  IN THE WORLD TODAY │
            └─────────────────────┘
                       │
                       ↓
                   BEYOND US
```

The first rule with this system of education is that *'learners must strictly play according to the 'book' in order to pass the test set by their teachers.'*

In effect educators and society see the learner as an empty bottle to be filled. Once filled up they expect these 'containers' to deliver accordingly as a condition for passing their test and graduating. There are few advantages but many disadvantages to this type of education.

Advantages include:-

- Less work or creativity required on the part of the teacher or learner
- Manageable learners who present fewer or no challenge
- Teachers can expect respect and enjoy power
- Very little or no challenge from learners
- Operative just within the lower level of learning taxonomy with very little to do by the teacher or learner
- Teaching materials including notes, materials, textbooks or methods that can be re-used many times with no need for change.

First rule with LIKE US system:

'learners must strictly go according to the 'book' in order to pass the test set by their teachers.'

Furthermore, the 'Like Us,' system of education is in most cases, in harmony with society or prevailing cultures. It reflects existing practices where community leaders or elders are to be heard and obeyed and not to be challenged, reminding us of the old adage that 'a child is to be seen and not be heard'. It is seen as non-threatening and therefore an attractive proposition.

Unfortunately however, this system of education is dangerously limited in its lack of capacity to produce real independent thinkers, creators, inventors and problem solvers.

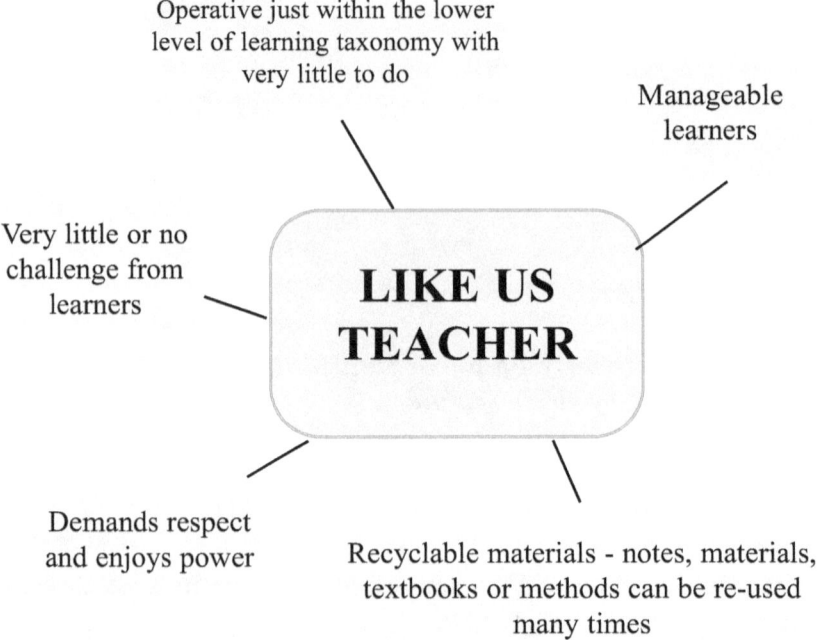

Organogram of Like Us Teacher

Disadvantages of Like Us, system of education

Like Us system is best described as passive [chalk and talk] education and for that reason carries with it several disadvantages including the potential for turning learners into:
 - Passive citizens lacking motivation
 - People that lack problem solving skills and creativity
 - Citizens that lack the skills required of a modern society
 - People that depend on government or society to solve their problems
 - Those that become power hungry and power corrupt and, would resist other views or anyone challenging them
 - People that are easily brainwashed, persuaded or misled

- People with little vision and practically no foresight
- People that turn to crime, inspiring fear or terror
- People that are adamant and resistant to change

The biggest limitation to this system of education is society. Neither the teacher nor the learner is able to see beyond the teacher or existing society. In their communities or even at work places, they dare not express their views, as this is seen as either a taboo within the culture or disrespect to authority. There is little or no incentive for independent thinking and creativity. All must tow the line of their leaders or face the consequences. In effect the learner is schooled to be like the teacher at their best and not strive to achieve beyond the capabilities of or challenge the teacher or society.

Unfortunately where learners are not given the opportunity to excel themselves to be inventive, creative and problem solvers, society is deprived of 'Gold Minds' capable of creating opportunities for all and bringing about progress.

The sad reality is that, this kind of education prevails in most parts of the world even today. There is probably a strong case for investigating a correlation between underdevelopment and this kind of education. Maybe, there is an even stronger case for testing the hypothesis that most poor countries are suffering not for the lack of education but the abundance of passive education that gives birth to dysfunctional citizens.

> **'Most poor countries are suffering not for the lack of education but the abundance of passive education** that gives birth to dysfunctional citizens. '

Examples of the, Like Us, system of education

As a product of this system of education, I can share my own experiences as well as those of others, by way of examples or as case studies under the following categories:

- Breeding fear
- Cultural Expectations
- Teacher knows it all
- Teacher is always right
- Thou shall not challenge an adult's opinion
- Thou shall not think beyond the Box
- To "obey" is better than to "challenge"
- The Powerful against the Powerless

Breeding fear

During both my primary and secondary education in Africa every school day began with the cane.
To start with we had school assemblies where those pupils that were perceived as rule-breakers would normally be called out and punished in front of the whole school.
The rules could be anything from lateness to school, not brushing your teeth, having long finger nails, not ironing your clothes with starch, forgetting to comb your hair, not bringing a cane to school to make up for the depleting stock of teacher's canes. Accordingly, breaking these rules was punishable by caning and public humiliation in front of the whole school.

This ritual humiliation almost every morning would be followed by the normal school periods where beating (or caning – to be precise), became part of the lesson for those having difficulties with learning.

We were expected to get 10 out of 10 in every exercise or face another caning ordeal for not delivering to the expectation of the teacher. This was irrespective of ability or whether the pupil understood the task or not.

As children this was a normal part of education. For us school was a place to endure pain and sometimes be humiliated. We learned through fear and yet we tried our best to live with this as part of daily living.

Indeed our teachers were people to be dreaded and worshipped who inspired learning through fear. Not only did they have too much power, most of them got used to abusing their powers to our misery and disadvantage.

As a result none of us dared to think for ourselves. Instead we were all pre-occupied with doing things to please our teachers and headmasters.

Again as a result of fear, we all became passive learners who learnt how to say 'Yes Sir' or 'Yes Madam' at all times.

Cultural Practices and Expectations

We lived in a society where children were supposed to be 'seen' and not 'heard.'
This was the practice within the community, at school, in the churches, or even in religious education within other faith groups [equally guilty of abusing power with threats, torture and abuse mainly in the form of physical punishment].

For this reason, any means for promoting children's silence and 'respect' for the adult's view had the support of the whole community including parents.
On the other hand views from learners which went beyond or challenged those of their teachers, masters, parents or adults, could be seen as unacceptable or taboo by all parties if those ideas were to be openly expressed.

Therefore, due to the immensity of the pressure on the young learner from within and outside school any potential for learners to be free and analytical thinkers was suppressed from the very beginning of childhood.

As a result, by the time the child reached adulthood, his or her thinking and analytical skills would have been extensively suppressed or underdeveloped giving rise to their inability to contribute their full potential to society. Generations of passive learners and clumsy teachers are bound to result in passive dysfunctional citizens [and their leaders] who just do as they are told without questioning.

In most cultures around the world, people are accustomed to telling others what to do and cannot understand or come to terms with hearing other views that may be different from theirs in their dealings with those who are more sophisticated than they are.

In effect their behaviour not only bears the hallmarks of the prevailing system of Like Us, education, it again exposes the weaknesses of the very system that gives rise to this kind of behaviour.

The teacher is always right
Rule Number One in the Like Us system of education is:
- The teacher is always right
Rule Number Two is:
- Whenever the learner thinks the teacher is wrong they should refer to Rule Number One
Prof Ken Evans 2007 [Ex-Professor of Educational Psychology University of London]
[Quote from his lecture to ITC London students based on his review of Gold Minds]

Again in cultures where doing as you are told is a sign of obedience and indeed the kind that has everyone's approval it would not come as a surprise for this kind of inherent weakness to be taken advantage of by foreign partners when it comes to negotiating terms for trade and international relations and diplomacy.

In effect, a Like Us, system of education preserve cultural practices and expectations to the detriment of growth and development.

Teacher Knows it All [chalk and talk] education

The teacher usually comes to the lesson with chalk in one hand and his notes in the other – unchanged for 20 years. There are often very little or no teaching or learning resources apart from the chalk and the blackboard. The teacher then talks and chalks throughout the lesson. They do this in an attempt to relate to the learner all the knowledge on the subject. In the end the learner is given notes, supposedly the blueprint of knowledge on that subject and passing the test.

In these lessons there is usually little differentiation or engagement with the learners in the discovery of knowledge or understanding. There is very little incentive for any critical and analytical thinking. This is because the teacher is seen by all as a powerful figure with encyclopaedic knowledge, who cannot go wrong and must therefore be obeyed.

These rules are set by teachers and also by society as a whole. Learners are not told directly but they are taken for granted, and never challenged.

'To obey is better than to challenge'
Instead of considering learners with thinking and analytical skills as potential asset to society, they can be seen as threats or anti establishment by systems that are tuned to make learners conform.

Unfortunately the Like Us, system of education is designed to gag these learners or fail those who refuse to conform to expectations.
We are therefore now faced with a situation where most learners with the potential for changing their world for the better either go underground or remain mute and shelve their talents in their quest for survival both within and beyond school.

The Powerful against the Powerless

Like Us, systems can be powerfully regimented, run by people or simply individuals over those who happen to fall within their jurisdiction.
To start with, those perceived as powerful will usually set their own standards and enforce these on others, misguided or not.

Guided or totally misguided and yet they are individually so powerful that in some cases it is necessary for them to crush anyone who dares to disobey. It is likely that this system dates back to the years of colonising European powers. Most of what we see today bears the hallmarks or echoes of many traits of colonisation, with key stakeholders fighting to protect and maintain strategic interest.

During the days of colonisation competition among the colonial masters from Europe meant that a, Like Us, system of education become a crucial weapon for colonial supremacy and control. Sometimes it led to some colonies relinquishing their language, culture and civilisation in favour of those of their colonial masters.

By the time of independence, the many years of colonisation had brought with it Western education, civilisation, culture and attitudes as those that had transformed these colonies to be like their masters. The result is that post-colonial governments find it almost impossible to be truly independent of their masters.

However, Like Us, systems are not only limited to ex-colonies and Third World countries. In the UK some educational establishment and institutions enjoy enormous power as a result of more than half of the world wanting British education. By operating a, 'Like Us', system, there seems to be a continuation of the powers which they enjoyed over their colonies under colonisation.

With demand from all over the world it is estimated that education is one of the biggest revenue generators for the UK. For this reason some individuals and institutions with authority and access to control in education in the UK will close down any schools, colleges, universities or institutions that fail to conform to their standards. Not only these, they dictate the price of British education to the rest of the world in a way that leaves no room for bargaining.

Among these institutions are individuals who truly enjoy exercising these powers and humiliating people with years of experience in education to the extent of making them jobless overnight if they do not sing to their tune or meet the requirements they impose.

In effect there is every reason to suggest that most of the, Like Us, systems seen in the world today are an indication of how the colonial masters did business with their subjects. In a way, that leaves them with no other alternative than for them to follow their colonial masters. Most probably this is their main reason behind their choice of 'Like Them' system of education.

Like Them, system of education

CHAPTER 02

02

The Like Them, model is based on the philosophy that if only a struggling system can somehow adopt the other seemingly successful model, then everything will be fine. In other words, let struggling nations adopt Western models of education as a way out of their problems. This kind of ideology has driven many to adopt and operate either the apparently successful British, American or European systems of education.

The biggest danger of this approach is that while the architects of the so-called Western education struggle to meet their own local or national needs and aspirations, these may have little or no relevance within a foreign context.

Yet the psychological effect of having these labels is dominant across the world, with nations and governments boasting of their education, based and run on Western principles. This is all very well, but what exactly does this mean? What have they achieved and what do they hope it will deliver in the long run?

We have a big problem here with people claiming to operate systems without any clear definitions and whose dynamics are determined by local or national needs or in some cases what their competitors are doing.

Disadvantage of the Like Them, system of education

The disadvantages of claiming to operate this system of education include the following:

- There is no conclusive definition in the West of the term education and this makes it impossible for subscribers to know what exactly they are buying

- It is practically impossible to keep up with the pace of change in Western education without compromising local standards

- There is no evidence that Western educational policies designed to address a local or national need will be relevant in a foreign context

- Western educational policies may be too costly and in the end give little or no value for money

- They may be difficult to operate or deliver due to lack of resources and skills for delivery

- The curriculum may be culturally irrelevant, and not designed to meet the subscribers national aspirations

- It may lead to the erosion of national values and identity where limits are not defined

If the disadvantages of claiming to operate this system of education are valid and so overwhelming, why is the whole world queuing up for this kind of education or label?

There appears to be three main reasons for such a claim which are mainly psychological, political, and economic.

1. Psychological and political reasons for the Western model

The most dominant reason for promoting Western education is prestige. To most people, it looks great to be seen as westernised in their own countries, after years of studying British history or watching Hollywood movies.

These nations are a great source of admiration to generations, and thus it makes sense both psychologically and politically to identify with them. For this reason they seem inclined to buying their education just as they buy other commodities such as jeans, trainers, or M&S sweaters.

The only difference is that whereas the manufacturers of jeans and trainers have the customer in mind, and will endeavour to design their products to include foreign markets accordingly, those who put in place Western education operate on a "One Size Fits All" basis.

However, in doing so they leave their customers with no option than to buy products that may not fit, for the sake of the label.

Economic Reasons

The cost of inventing a new system of education unique to a nation's situation may be too much and not affordable for poor countries.
Therefore, to save money, some nations prefer to buy education that may be relatively cheaper for them. They may see it as a catalyst for trade and international relations.

There are those who believe that it is vital for good trade and international diplomacy. Though these countries are politically independent from colonisation, this is hardly educational or ideological emancipation.

As a result we are left with a situation whereby for these nations the only one source of hope is to cling on to their colonial masters and go along with anything that bears the masters label.

Examples of Like Them education

- Subscribing to Education: Third World countries subscribe to what they perceive to be British, American, or European systems of education

- Colonial Education: Third World nations learning about British or American history, literature, or systems of government

- Psychological Education: Some schools in Third World and developing countries claiming to be British or American Schools

However most of these systems portray themselves, often very little of what they provide can be justified as being British.

In conclusion, those who claim to have a British education, for example, should endeavour to be more specific about what this entails. This should perhaps enable us to understand their motives as to what they hope to achieve in their countries with their version of Western education.

Beyond Us system of education

CHAPTER 03

03

A leading educationalist whose work and philosophy has helped shape the policies of advanced nations for almost a century describes the object of true education as enabling learners to be inventors, creators, and innovators.

Jean Piaget, amongst others, worked with the philosophy that the human mind has a characteristic or quality called intelligence that is measurable and capable of developing for the purposes of solving complex problems.

Education is, therefore, best seen as a means of enabling learners to develop as individuals in order to push society ahead by creating new opportunities.
This kind of thinking has become very popular among Western nations like France, Germany, Britain, and America in their competition for global supremacy. It dates back as far back as 1905, when educational philosophers and psychologists such as Alfred Binet started talking about man's ability to measure and nurture human intelligence. Since then educators and psychologists have tried methods aimed at developing thinking and problem-solving skills in learners.

This is normally approached in ways that allow and challenge them to be free and independent. They do his with the hope of guiding learners to be creative and inventive in their thinking and approach to challenges in life.

There have been several contributors to this process. Among these are those who have made sure that it became an intrinsic part of Western education. For example, Professor Benjamin Bloom from Chicago University and his team of leading thinkers in education devised a model for explaining this using the idea best understood as a stairway with six major steps to learning.

In their model the six steps are rough approximations, not fixed absolutes, and correspond to other systems or learning hierarchies that have been devised. But the beauty is that Bloom's taxonomy was created for categorising levels of abstraction, and questions that commonly occur in educational settings. For this reason it is easily understood and capable of being widely applied.

These are designed to test or measure quantitative and qualitative learning outcomes of:
1) New knowledge and skills acquired by the learner
2) The level or depth of understanding
3) Ability as well as quality of application
4) Analytical skills of the learner
5) Learners' ability and skill of synthesis
6) Learners' ability to evaluate

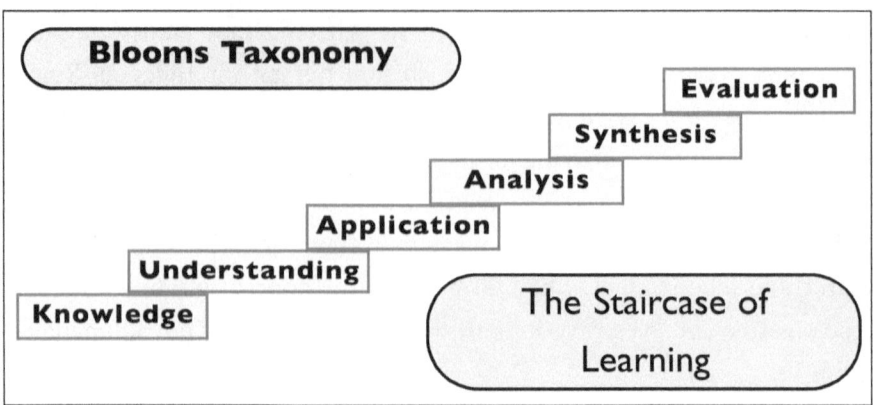

The taxonomy provides a useful structure with which to categorise test questions, since professors and teachers will characteristically ask questions within a particular levels, and if one can determine the level of questions that will appear in examinations, students and learners will be able to study using appropriate strategies.

This model is one example of an open-ended approach to education that places no limits on learners' abilities to achieve.

In countries where learners are, schooled, to play by the book, it is customary to see the majority of learners and graduates [including their teachers and educators] operating at Level One of the taxonomy, namely that of knowledge.

These so-called graduates have been careful to play by the book to the extent that they have acquired knowledge over the years that are hardly applied. The lack of skill for application leaves very little room for analytical thinking, synthesis and evaluation. They know and can indeed reproduce all the facts according to the book, but, unfortunately that is where their education ends.

Throughout their education they have been deprived of the skills of critical thinking, analysis, application, creativity and the synthesis. They have indeed not been prepared in any way to become part of the solution to the new and increasingly complex challenges faced by modern society.

However, in developed and advanced countries alike, the key to progress is the proportion of their population (graduates and workforce) that operate along the whole spectrum or levels of the taxonomy.

Beyond Us, systems of education, aim, at creating a platform for learner skills and independence in acquiring, understanding and knowledge application. It also enables the learner in acquiring and applying analytical skills which should lead to real problem solving and evaluation.

Where each cycle aims at producing new lessons or higher levels of knowledge, it also provides the basis for the opportunity of the synthesizing of an even newer and higher level of questioning.

The result is that we have a significant number of learners and eventually members of society geared for overcoming challenges and creating opportunities for others.

> Where each cycle is aimed at new lessons and discovery it provides the opportunity for another new but higher cycle, which begins with a new and possibly higher level of knowledge.

Beyond Us systems of education therefore provide a framework for society or even a nation for that matter to be equipped to deal with and overcome new and complex challenges as well as to lay foundations for progress and prosperity within a nation.

Any nation or people that would like to realise the true benefits of education needs to move towards preparing their generation to look at as well as think beyond their existing generation.

In doing so, we all need the benefit of hindsight and would suggest that it can be achieved in the following ways:

- By studying the success stories of other nations such as Great Britain, and the reasons behind their success
- To critically review existing practices with the view of learning new lessons

- To work towards a new educational framework capable of addressing local, national and international challenges

In effect, this is about striking the right balance between nature (our natural and human resources) and nurture (our ability to build our human capacity to functional levels within society such that they are capable of as well as committed to building a healthy and sustainable society, where there are opportunities for everyone).

It is almost common knowledge that developed countries have a significant number of their citizens operating at the functional level where they contribute to the building of the nation's wealth.

For me the greatest challenge for those wanting to keep the British or so-called Western education is the ability to keep up with the pace of change in their educational systems, and weigh up their cost against their effectiveness or value for money.

The accelerating pace of change by way of policy and practice within the UK alone makes it almost impossible to come out with clear definition of what education is about other than an attempt to address an existing or current concern within the UK.

There are several ideas and many experiments taking place all with the aim of trying to improve on standards in education, creativity and skills. Indeed, for every nation, this drive should hold the key to progress in striking gold between nature and nurture.

This is one side of the argument.

The challenge is our ability to question our motives or rationale for buying Western education. Together these will, I believe give buyers some serious work to do if they are to justify the benefits to poor or developing nations.

I believe that there are lessons for all parties to be learnt. To begin with those who continue to spend their hard earned national income on Western education may be persuaded to begin a search for a better deal from their suppliers. On the other hand, their Western counterparts who may genuinely like to help to bring about development would be pleased for providing value for money.

Again, if the common stake is education then the buyers from poor nations need to be equipped to know and analyse what they are buying and how to get value for money. In the like manner, those marketing Western education probably need more education themselves about their clients and how best to address their needs.

It is only by doing this that both parties can demonstrate their seriousness and commitment in addressing national and global challenges and **MAKING POVERTY HISTORY**.

We hope that this kind of education will begin somehow with the rest of this book which is aimed at discovering the British educational journey and how Western education has played a role in development. Perhaps we may learn or discover how this might possibly transfer to other nations.

British Education?

CHAPTER 04

04

Most countries in the developing and Third World boast of operating a Western education, especially British or American.

However what do they mean by this exactly? Is it to do with school structure, textbooks, the curriculum planning, delivery, implementation, evaluation or policy?

What exactly do schools or for that matter governments and policy makers mean when they claim to be operating a Western education? Indeed, given that in the UK alone there is no such definitive term or system, it immediately raises questions as to what those making those claims are really talking about.

Since the war Britain's education has been on such a rollercoaster ride that almost every new decade or government has brought with it significant change leading to an almost entirely new brand of education. The result is that there has been no less than twenty major changes in British education since the war, all of which are either in accordance with political or ideological inclinations or seen as a necessity in responding to local or national needs.

This being the case then, what is the rationale in operating a Western education designed to meet local needs and having little to do with the outside buyer?

Indeed, how do we choose the right brand of Western education and justify operating this kind of education?

On other hand, how do our policy makers justify bringing in a Western education in which they have not been involved or consulted during its formation, and for that reason may have little or no connection with local needs?

This is not to say that there can be no justification in importing some aspects of British or Western education.

For one thing, the apparent successes of the Western world since the war, leaves no doubt of the existence of lessons of good practice that are needed by those looking for ways to similarly develop their own countries or economies.

For some reason, even before the war Europe and the whole of the west had competed on the platform of education, with the belief that 'good' education was the key to progress and development.

It does not therefore come as a surprise to see the rest of the world following their former colonial masters and queuing for Western education.

However, in doing so, one may wonder why Western education falls short of achieving the same objects outside its borders after all these years. We need to look again critically at the difference between labels and reality and to search for real answers; to pause and ask serious questions as to what is wrong with our education today and how best to address any pitfalls.

If education is not about problem solving and improving the quality of lives, then is it not a waste of time and resources? We need the kind of education that will help overcome problems and improve lives within and beyond our communities.

We need to pause and ask serious questions as to what is wrong with our education today and how best to address any pitfalls.

What is probably also needed is a critical dialogue between those who formulate and supply Western education and those who subscribe to this kind of education. Without such critical engagement, any poor or developing country that happens to subscribe to Western education will find it difficult to reap the kind of benefits seen in the West.

Defining British Education

CHAPTER 05

05

Defining British education is virtually an impossible task. This is because a lot of years and effort has gone into its history and evolution, making it almost impossible to describe what it is exactly in few words.

To begin with, there apparently is no unified history in British education until after probably the Second World War, when the government took the idea of education in Britain wholly on board as part of the Welfare State reforms. Indeed for the first time education became a significant agenda of government leading to the introduction of the 1944 Education Act.

However, Britain in some ways has had the advantage of inheriting some level of civilisation through their own colonial masters, the Romans. Not only have they benefited from colonisation, there has also been the spur of competition with their European and American counterparts because of industrial and economic gains as well as global supremacy.

During this era there came a moment where the need for intelligent people became foremost on the minds of certain individuals. There were some like the French psychologist Alfred Binet [1857-1911], who believed that intelligence could be measured. However, there were others, such as Jean Piaget [1896-1980] who believed that beyond measuring intelligence, the mind was capable of growth and development. Invariably, most of Piaget's work in the area of developing thinking or cognitive development has had a great influence in Western education and thinking generally, and Britain in particular.

Though not politicians themselves, their work continues to shape the minds of policy makers in the West. For one thing, these are the people who by their own experience can make sense of the philosophy and background thinking, as well as its implementation. For us, in trying to make sense of what is currently going on in Western education and particularly in Britain, we need to look briefly historically at how education has evolved, as well as at the key contributors and what they believed in.
As far as Britain is concerned, certain individuals played key roles that need considering, especially when it comes to making sure that thinking skills or cognitive development featured in the curriculum.

Among other things, they set it upon themselves to evolve and experiment with a Western education aimed at enabling learners to reach their highest possible level of creativity as part of the process of learning.

Behind their strategies was the belief that the mind is capable of developing beyond normal expectations, through organised and systematic exercise called thinking skills.

Since its invention, the practice has been a common feature of British and indeed Western education, in a way that up to the present has been unique to the West. Though no one has ever claimed any credit for this, the results of years of experimenting with this method of education, one might argue, has contributed to what may now be perceived as the essential ingredient contributing to Western success or development.

If this is a valid observation, then it leads to the question: why is the rest of the world not getting similar results from what they believe to be a truly Western education?

Not only is it necessary for this question to be asked generally, but it is also necessary that it be directed at the overseas equivalents of the Blairs, Browns, Camerons, Obamas, Gates, Blanksons, the Hillarys, and Winfreys, in Africa, or India or Bangladesh, where the potential for growth is stunted by political ineptitude. In other words, how do we educate future generations with the knowledge and skills to overcome the challenges of development, and to create wealth and opportunities for others through skilful thinking creativity and appropriate action?

On the question of 'nature' and 'nurture', Third World countries need to seriously consider what is needed to turn their natural resources and human capacity into wealth creation just as Great Britain succeeded in turning a land of 'coal mines' into the world's leading 'gold reserves' probably through the nurturing of 'Gold Minds' over the years.

However without discovering what went wrong with Africa's inability to maintain their 'gold mines and reserves', the continent risks losing sight of the significance of nurturing its human capacity to recover or rediscover some of its 'lost gold'.

We aim at the possibility of exploring true skills and methods in Western education with the view of unearthing talents in the underdeveloped world, and to dispel the myth that global poverty is due to lack of education. The real problem may have more to do with abundance of poor or wrong education than the lack of it. Again, our work is based on the hypothesis:

"The biggest problem facing the Third World today is intellectual poverty".

Years of passive education, we believe, have produced generations of school leavers incapable of playing their role in society, in overcoming life's challenges and creating opportunities for others. What is needed is a careful study of other success stories to see if there are lessons to be learnt.

To our knowledge, one of such journeys of interest to us starts with the story of two people independently journeying across the Atlantic, and, by some strange coincidence, both being committed to improving the lives of others through the intellectual enrichment of young people within schools. Their work together spells a brief period of history in the development of thinking skills that can be found in our next chapter.

History of thinking skills development and the beginnings of Beyond Us Education

CHAPTER 06

06

The development of thinking skills teaching in schools has been strongly influenced by the work of Reuven Feuerstein and Matthew Lipman. They among others have pioneered different approaches to teaching thinking, and their ideas have subsequently influenced the development of other programmes.

Work of Feuerstein and Lipman have had a boost over the years with contributions from leading educationists such as Benjamin Bloom. As teachers have applied these approaches there has been an exchange of ideas and techniques between the different methods and an increasing emphasis on how the approaches work so that they can be integrated into teaching more generally.
In this section we aim to provide some background information about the history, evolution and development of thinking skills programmes and approaches to teaching and learning in some Western countries. We hope that the information will help to clarify the intentions of those responsible for the early development of such approaches and explain the way that their thinking has influenced subsequent work in thinking skills. There will be attempts to look at models and classifications within the school of thinking skills and their legacy on British education. We hope that in the end a platform would be created for a debate on the true definition of British or Western education.

Reuven Feuerstein

After the World War II, a large number of young people flooded into Israel from Europe and North Africa. Many of them had suffered traumatic early experiences and many more had not experienced an upbringing which had provided them with consistent family or cultural influences. On traditional psychometric tests, such as IQ tests or standardised tests of achievement, many of those youngsters scored so badly as to appear uneducable.

Rather than simply accept this conclusion and close the door on any kind of recovery, Reuven Feuerstein, who was engaged in trying to integrate young immigrants, devised ways of finding out exactly what cognitive functions they were deficient in; how they could be helped to develop these functions, and what each individual's potential for learning was.

Feuerstein developed a set of techniques that helped these learners succeed in subsequent tests. These methods were termed 'dynamic', in the sense that they were studying the process of learning and the change that took place, as opposed to 'static' traditional testing methods. Feuerstein favoured the dynamic approach with the view that such a process was much more likely to predict how a person might then learn in the future as opposed to their current performance.

Together with his colleagues he developed a Learning Potential Assessment Device [LPAD] for measuring an individual's intellectual change, known as 'cognitive modifiability'.

Not only did they develop tools for assessment, other instruments of learning such as 'Instrumental Enrichment' [IE] were devised as means by which an adult could intervene and help children's learning processes. Together these became tools for tackling different underlying difficulties of functioning and instruments for enabling learning with individuals, groups or whole classes.

Groups or classes were generally preferred, in that they gave opportunities for learning through discussion and through witnessing other children's learning processes.

These instruments were used in such a way that as learning became more complex, the same concepts and skills were re-introduced, at higher levels of conceptualisation, according to a "planned spiral curriculum". Many of Feuerstein ideas have influenced work on teaching thinking skills, in particular his innovative theory of mediated learning.

Matthew Lipman and Philosophy for Children

Another important pioneer in what the United States termed the Critical Thinking movement, also talked about in the UK as the thinking skills, is the American philosopher, Matthew Lipman. Originally a university philosophy professor, Lipman was unhappy at what he saw as poor thinking in his students. He became convinced that something was wrong with the way they had been taught in school when they were younger. They seemed to have been encouraged to learn facts and to accept authoritative opinions, but not to think for themselves.

As a result he founded the Institute for the Advancement of Philosophy for Children (I.A.P.C.) at Montclair State College, New Jersey where he and his colleagues subsequently developed material for use in schools, aimed at helping young people (from 6 year-olds to late adolescents) to think.

The programme called Philosophy for Children was based on Lipman's basic convictions that children are natural philosophers, in the sense that they view the world about them with curiosity and wonder. That is all that is needed as a starting-point for enquiry, which can legitimately be termed 'philosophical.

The I.A.P.C. has produced a number of novels, into every page of which, strange and anomalous points have been woven. As a class reads a page, with the teacher, the text encourages them to raise queries.

These queries form the basis of guided discussions. The teacher does not try to control what questions are asked, since it is the children's curiosity which needs to be tapped, in order to promote active participation and active learning. The text, itself, steers the children's questions into certain areas, suitable for exploration, and the novels provide a model of philosophical enquiry, in that they involve fictional children engaging in argument, debate, discussion and exploratory thinking.

Lipman firmly believes that levels of sophistication in thinking are arrived at by practice in appropriate forms of thinking. Ironically this was in contradiction to views by the Swiss psychologist Jean Piaget that sophistication in thinking was part of biological or other stages of development. As soon as children can speak, they are using reasoning, according to Lipman.

Both Feuerstein and Lipman, though from very different starting-points, hold a similar belief in children's abilities. They consider that through thinking exercises and activities learners can exceed the predicted level of competence which psychometric or school-based tests may have suggested is their limit.

Thinking skills in the UK: More Examples of 'Beyond Us' Education

CHAPTER 07

07

The pioneering work of Feuerstein and Lipman, as well as other leading figures such as Edward de Bono, has inspired a wide range of work in the UK. Programmes developed along the lines of thinking skills within mainstream UK over the years have included such as:
- TASC (Thinking Actively in a Social Context)
- ACTS (Activating Children's Thinking Skills)
- Thinking through Geography: Leat, 1998
- Thinking Through Primary Teaching: Higgins, 2001
- Thinking Through History: Fisher, 2002
- Cognitive Acceleration Through Science Education (CASE)
- Thinking Together

Most programmes and approaches acknowledge the importance of language, articulation and discussion. For some, such as 'Thinking Together', it forms both the underpinning rationale as well as the pedagogy. Philosophy for Children has also been developed extensively in the UK and uses a structured approach to classroom discussion as a key element in the approach.

The influence of Robert Fisher in developing classroom resources to develop a community of enquiry is particularly as significant, as the work of Karin Murris and the Society for the Advancement of Philosophical Enquiry in Education (SAPERE).

The philosophical category reflects the tradition of Matthew Lipman and the development of Philosophy for Children; the cognitive work of Reuven Feuerstein (and other psychological theories) as well as the impact of teaching approaches. Edward de Bono's influence, amongst others, can be identified in the brain-based approaches. There are clear similarities in each of the categories. In effect, the makers of Western education had a lot in common, in their belief in the elasticity of the human mind.

1944 Educational Act

This Act laid the foundation for education today, for decades contained in it its recommendations which dominated the education system in England and Wales. The main ones were derived from Cyril Burt's idea that intelligence tests could be used to assess a child's mental ability by the age of 12.
Reports by Hadow (1926}, Spens (1938) and Norwood (1943) claimed that it was possible to sort children into groups based on their intelligence and to allocate them to the appropriate school. This line of thinking has influenced policies such as setting or grouping of children into below average, average, and above average as opposed to mix ability grouping.

The 1944 Act introduced the following changes:
- County councils to organise education within their areas into primary, secondary and further stages;
- Free compulsory secondary education to be available for all children between 11 and 15
- Compulsory school-leaving age to rose from 14 to 15 (in 1945, and later to 16)
- Local authorities to provide schools meals, free milk and regular medical inspections,
- The ministry of education was created to control and direct the implementation of education policy.

Thinking Skills in the Curriculum

In the UK, five main aspects of thinking skills are embedded in the curriculum for Key Stages 1 and 2 along the lines of:
- Information Processing Skills
- Reasoning Skills
- Enquiry Skills
- Creative Thinking Skills
- Evaluation Skills

It is hoped that **Information Processing** skills will enable pupils to locate and collect relevant information, to sort, classify, sequence, compare, contrast, and to analyse part/whole relationships (QCA 2000).

Reasoning skills on the other hand should enable pupils to give reasons for opinions and actions, to draw inferences and make deductions, to use precise language to explain what they think, and to make judgments and decisions informed by reasons or evidence (QCA 2000). Reasoning involves reaching decisions and making judgments or choices e.g. we may decide one solution will not work while another solution takes us a step forward. We then set out to prove or explain why that solution works. Errors or misjudgements in reasoning then become apparent. It is hoped that in the process learners are able to decode and make sense of a text or proposition, and to gain and make use of knowledge gained from these through literal interpretation, deduction and inference.

Enquiry skills enable pupils to ask relevant questions, to pose and define problems, to plan what to do and how to research, to predict outcomes and anticipate responses, to test conclusions and improve ideas (QCA 2000). Frameworks are therefore focused on developing these skills where the focus is upon exploring and investigating patterns, rules and conventions in the structure of language or the curriculum.

Creative thinking skills enable pupils to generate and extend ideas, to suggest hypotheses, to apply imagination, and to look for alternative innovative outcomes (QCA, 2000). Creativity is generally considered as an element of thinking which is closely linked to reasoning and enquiry skills in terms of the learner's ability to explore and invent patterns and connections. They incorporate roots of generalisation, investigation and rule construction, as well as aspects of imaginative and logical thinking in empowering the learner with the capacity to suppose, pretend, adopt roles and suspend.

Evaluation skills enable pupils to evaluate information, to judge the value of what they read, hear and do, to develop criteria for judging the value of their own and others' work or ideas, and to have confidence in their judgments. Evaluative skills develop from the early formation of preferences for books, materials, style, etc. to a more critical awareness of how these serve their differing purposes, based on the pupils' growing awareness of substance or their content and their related organisational features, the use of language for precision and effect their growing awareness of authors, styles and philosophy.
Teachers need to equip pupils with the relevant knowledge and technical language to analyse and conceptualise this critical awareness so that it becomes increasingly possible for pupils to transfer it from their reading, observation or judgments to their writing or presentation and to self-evaluate and refine their own work as well as appreciating the work of others.

In effect, just as education in the UK, though, Beyond Us education had its beginnings through the private sector or individual initiatives, it has over the years found its way into mainstream education and become popular among policy makers. As one leader puts it,

"......The human brain is like an orange fruit. Unless we prepared to squeeze or do some massaging to our brains through cognitive thinking or learning activities, it is impossible to get all the juice".
        Rev. Jesse Jackson Sir. TV Broadcast Chicago August 2007

It looks as if those who realized this secret went ahead of the rest many years ago evolving systems aimed at squeezing as much brain juice as possible for the benefit of society.

It may be the case that those who struggle to catch up with the West today as well as those aspiring to develop need to explore seriously the benefits and possibilities of more brain massaging among their people. However these need to be tested along the lines described, and within the context of enabling people to think beyond themselves with the aim of befitting society as a whole.

Evidence-based results and progression in British Education

CHAPTER 08

08

On balance, research findings have vindicated such claims that development of thinking skills is key to progress. In 2001 results of projects using IE, and IAPC's literature, carried out by an independent testing agency, on over 2,000 children showed that when compared with control children, they made large gains, after a year, for Maths, larger gains for English and even larger ones for reasoning.

These results for Philosophy for Children have been replicated in other countries, such as Iceland (Sigurborsdottir, 1998) and other subjects such as science (Sprod, 1998).
It should be noted that gains on specific assessment procedures, which test performance on items not specifically taught for in the thinking skills programmes, also provide evidence for the modifiability of intelligence, as well as for transfer of learned skills.
In effect, thinking skills developed in one sphere of education has ripple effects in other areas. These results vindicate these philosophers who set up a standard for education aimed at cognitive development, as well as group and individual work that encourages free and independent but quality thinking and contribution. They were vehemently opposed to encouraging children to learn facts and accept authoritative opinions but not think to for themselves.

The Challenge

If encouraging children to learn facts and accept authoritative opinions, but not to think for themselves, became more or less an abomination in Britain in the course of their history, why is this kind of practice still prevalent in parts of Africa and the rest of the world that boast of British education, even up to university level?
Are these nations getting the real thing or instead a counterfeit? For those who are adamant about their version of British education, how much of their world has it changed for the better due to their British or Western education?'
Almost 60 years after the war, the world still remains like the laboratory of that independent testing agency, where children in Western schools can be compared with those 2000 that had the chance to succeed through refined Western education. They in turn can be compared to their control counterparts in the rest of the world who for some strange reason, boast of British education while ironically, heavily dependent on encouraging children to learn facts and accept authoritative opinions but not to think for themselves.

In the Third World [as well as among some traditionalists in the West], education has always been seen as the process of identifying and selecting 'natural conformist or survivors' as opposed to 'enabling and empowering individuals and society to think and develop their potential'.
The practice of selecting 'conformists and survivors', however risks limiting all parties involved with the whole of society as a casualty. It is sad to say that very little [if any] of the revolutionary enabling aspects of British or Western education described in this book were exported beyond the shores of Britain or the West. For this reason the conformists approach whereby only those who meet the status quo matter to society is still prevalent.
In effect the teacher's role has always been to tell and make learners tow

their line of thinking, or else risk becoming casualties. Even in the twenty first century, the concept of the, 'teacher as an enabler', is almost non-existent or very thin in these countries.

A rapid transition is needed in our thinking and approach to education with the view of providing the necessary catch-up for those who lag behind. Probably this is best achieved by looking at some trends or progression in British education.

Progression in British education

British education has been through several transformations since the war, such that it makes it almost impossible to keep up with the pace of change. This confusion is not helped in any way by the fact that there have been several brands of British education exported before and since the war, starting from colonisation to post war and post independence as well as the modern day so-called modern British education.

What is more fascinating still is the fact that though the system has come under constant review due to perceived imperfection and intervention by governments. Despite all these, the market for British education has never experienced a downturn. There are always buyers ready to pay for anything thrown at them without pause for thought or reflection as long as it is British or from the West. The result is that British education is among the hottest selling commodities on the planet today. But at what price are they buying this product and where are the guarantees?

A benefit of hindsight is needed. This will require a brief look at what has happened in Britain before and since Second World War in an attempt to make sense of what is happening at the moment.

We hope to do this in an attempt to help the buyer of British or Western education to work out or have some idea of what they are buying and how they stand to benefit or lose.

British Education - A Long and Winding Road!

CHAPTER 09

09

British education has become many things. For besides being; the Western education in the British Isles it is also a product for sale on the international market. As such it is valued for its effectiveness in achieving educated individuals.

But it has not always been an enviable product as a social force shaping whole societies. Thus it has a history as a tortuous path of gradual development.

Until the early 19th nineteenth century, at the outset of the Industrial Revolution there was no education for the majority of children in Britain. Some of the movements which led to education were the result of early industrialisation, but were crucial in the overall direction of the British Western education.
For example, one of the effects of industrialisation was the massive population shift from the countryside to the new industrial towns. This was arguably the most dire period in British history. Indeed, this was the period of the Coal Mines!

The vast overcrowding, the long working hours in factories and mines, and the sudden frenzied increase in population placed a severe strain on the hitherto rural social system, and one of the consequences of this was the large numbers of orphaned and neglected children living on the streets. This pattern of population growth has been repeated throughout the world as an aspect of industrial development.

In England during early part of the nineteenth century and thereafter one way of dealing with this was to gather the children together and provide very basic education as a means of managing the problem. These were the Ragged Schools, whose teachers would collect the children from the streets in the morning, provide a cheap meal of thin porridge and then give them some basic education. From the various accounts of these schools we know that there were many well-intentioned and public spirited individuals who might be described as having a belief in education as a moral force. However in the main the purpose of the Ragged School was containment of the unwanted children.

As a result all of the early Education Acts of Parliament were attempts to fill up the gaps in educational provision for the poor. Any reading of how mass education became the responsibility of the state must take into account the competition between the various churches, the government's fears of the consequences of an unschooled population, (this was also a time of political revolution in Europe) and the need for an educated workforce. This was a heavy mix of social, political, religious, and economic pressures forcing the several governments of this period to act to gain control of education in Britain.

Education became one of the key issues in political debates. The **Revd W H Milman**, an Anglican clergyman summed it up in his article, *The Education of the People* published in the Quarterly Review (vol 78 - 1846)

'Sooner or later, popular education must be an affair of the State...not merely as making grants to different (religious) societies, and demanding the right to inspection over schools which receive such grants; but as establishing some system administered by an efficient and responsible

board....for providing masters to work on some well-matured plans, with books under a proper supervision, and paid, at least in great part, by the State...The schoolmaster must become a public functionary, duly qualified for his office, and under due control.`

To fully understand how the British education system developed, it is essential to read the various Education Acts from 1870 onwards, and also the various Parliamentary Commissions which addressed the various problems as they arose, but to do so in detail is very hard work!

Instead we can get a better feel of what was happening during this early phase of development from commentators of those times, especially from the novelist Charles Dickens. Most of his work paints a grim picture of British society adapting to the demands of industrialisation and especially the employment and education of young people.

In *Nicholas Nickleby* we can glimpse the meanness of the times in the portrayal of the wonderfully named brutal school, Dotheboys Hall where the children are:

'Pale and haggard faces, lank and bony figures, children with countenances of old men, deformities with irons upon their limbs, boys of stunted growth, and others long meagre legs would hardly bear their stooping bodies, all crowded on the view together; there were the bleared eye, the hare-lip, the crooked foot, and every ugliness or distortion that told of unnatural aversion conceived by parents for their offspring, or of young lives which, from the earliest dawn of infancy, had been one horrible endurance of cruelty and neglect'.

'There were little faces which should have been handsome, darkened with the scowl of sullen, dogged suffering; there was childhood with the light of its eye quenched, its beauty gone, and its helplessness alone remaining.'

Dickens wished to expose what he considered to be the abuses and failings of the system and his novels played an immeasurable part in persuading public opinion that the system had to change. And even when the system did change, Dickens lampooned the style of education, as being too much a system of Like Us. In the novel Hard Times, Mr Gradgrind is the champion of this restrictive form of education.

" Now what I want is, Facts. Teach these boys and girls nothing but Facts. Facts alone are wanted in life. Plant nothing else, and root out everything else. You can only form the minds of reasoning animals upon Facts: nothing will ever be of service to them."

Besides his novels, Dickens gave public speeches and published articles on education. He was also well acquainted with the middle-class fee-paying schools which emphasised a sense of loyalty, respect, duty and honour, and he saw these values as somehow underpinning a system that would enable all children to reach their potential regardless of their financial situation.

At the time Dickens was writing his novels, Britain was ruling the greatest empire in history, an empire where the sun never set. An empire won, against the competition of other European nations, by the sweat and courage of ordinary men schooled by the most rudimentary methods, led by officers from the upper echelons of British society whose common link was their educational background, Public schools such as Eton, Harrow and Rugby. The gap between officers and men was educational as much as social and economic; the main difference being that lower classes were schooled to follow their leaders and the upper classes were expected to think for themselves and lead from the front.

The tortuous route of British education absorbed ideas from many sources, including the idea that national supremacy depended on education. Before the end of the nineteenth century the British government became alarmed that Britain was losing its industrial lead in competition with other European countries. The improved teaching of science and technology became an important matter for Parliamentary debate and action. Teacher training and the curriculum also became key issues, and after 1944, the idea that all children should receive the appropriate education to meet their educational needs became an essential idea which became the hallmark of British education.

There is a common assumption that the democratising forces that have shaped modern British society are the direct consequence of the British education system. Certainly the independent character associated with British people is partly a consequence of the current Education System. However, British culture is shaped by many other social and political forces and it would be impossible to transfer all the aspects, even if it was deemed desirable to do so, to another part on the world.

But, for any developing nation intending to extend democratic rights and responsibilities to its citizens, there would be benefits from introducing the best of a very mixed system. This of course raises the question, what do we mean by the suggestion of, 'the best of British education?'.

British education is as susceptible as anything else to fashion and the whims of politicians. The flow of ideas and the changing challenges of a modern society require a system that can adapt and change without disturbing the learning of its cache. During the nineteen sixties the social changes produced a crop of ideas which challenged long-held assumptions about the nature of education.

One of the ideas that fitted well with the times was that education had become merely schooling, and that there was still a tendency to train individuals to become placid members of society, rather than individual social agents of change.

One of the continuing debates concerns the purpose of education. The politicians see it as the main socialising instrument for citizens to become useful members of society; a few see it as a benefit for the individual, who will become a more independent and able person; businessmen and commercial leaders see it as equipping their employees with skills which will add to their business success.

Other societies which feel the global pressures to compete in the global market-place view their own education systems as inadequate and look in the direction of more successful countries.
Among them are the countries which were once ruled by Britain. Their Western education is part of their inheritance as colonies, but even the best of these are hopelessly out of date in their curriculum, their teaching and learning strategy, pedagogy, and their examination system.
What appears on the surface to be British education is an obsolete version of something which has failed to embrace a learning culture of continuous change.

Nurturing future Minds as Agents of Change

CHAPTER 10

10

The die is cast in favour of British education for most nations and individuals on this planet, and it is almost certain to stay with us for generations to come.
Considering the certainty for this market and the potential effects upon all parties involved, we believe that every attempt is needed to make this system of education work somehow for at least a significant number of people from both inside and outside the box who invest in Western education.

As one can glean from the pages of this book, British education is by no means a perfect system. It is at best a system trying to define itself through rigorous experimentation by British people for British people. Ironically, while they struggle with their own system exclusively for their people, outside buyers are never in short supply.

We would reiterate our belief that the biggest attraction for British education is psychological. For an outsider, British education is a means of respect and good job prospects within and beyond their own borders. The result is that unfortunately we have many foreigners with British education that only exists on paper such that they go back to their countries as dysfunctional as their fellow countrymen irrespective of their so-called British education.

In a recent discussion with other practitioners, practitioner in a Third

World country argued that almost all their leaders were either educated in Europe or America and yet in most cases were as dysfunctional and corrupt as those who never travelled outside their country.

If this is the picture across Africa and the Third World then there is something seriously wrong that needs addressing.

For one thing it dashes the hopes and aspirations of their sponsors who would have paid a lot of money with the hope of creating a functional society capable of overcoming challenges as opposed to depleting natural resources.

If inability to produce functional citizens or members of society is deemed as failure, then someone must be willing to carry some of the blame.

There are those who blame Western educational institutions for their lack of understanding and inability to equip the African or Third World citizens or participants to overcome their national challenges. In other words insufficient time and effort is devoted by these institutions to understand and help equip or change the African through education, to the point at which they are able to help themselves. Indeed, there are those who remain cynical about the genuineness of the apparent will of the West to promote true and appropriate education outside their region.

However there are also those who would argue that there may be the case of the West being able to 'lead the horse to the water but lacking the power to persuade it to drink.'

In other words it is possible to acquire Bloom's education of knowledge, understanding and all the skills for application, analysis, synthesis and evaluation. However, if the home environment is not ready for their rigorous application, they can remain just ideas on a piece of paper or bottled in an individual.

In an environment where success is measured by the number of academic, cultural or religious titles to one's name, or the number of houses, cars, private jets and wives, as opposed to opportunities created for others, there is a real problem. And this includes the temptation to shelve knowledge and skills acquired in favour of these things most cherished by society.

Unfortunately, in Africa and most of the Third World, this kind of expectation by society has become the greatest catalyst or agent for depletion of national resources. In other words unless there are serious attempts to address these misconceptions which lie at the heart of our beliefs and practices, it is impossible to see any light at the end of the tunnel.

Africans need great lessons from history and from those who explored the world with their bid to turn their nation from a land of coal to a land of gold. They probably need to give some credit to the British as well as take lessons from their ability to turn ordinary coal into a great asset, when the need arose for steam or locomotive engineering as a bed rock to industrialisation.

Perhaps the first lesson that can be learnt from this is that a true Gold Mind is determined to overturn the desperate situation at home and bring hope to others through their labour, sacrifice and innovation. Their charity begins at home and reaches beyond their borders to others in similar situations.

The road to recovery in Africa and the Third World should therefore begin with a campaign for change. However change will not happen without winning hearts and minds of the people and all stakeholders and agents involved in the recovery of these nations. A miracle is needed on the road to recovery, which should involve the following:

- Strong and visionary leadership
- Clear programme for change towards a truly functional society with everyone contributing their bit
- Campaign for hearts and minds to be behind the programme
- A good and contextualised Beyond Us Western education and Skills programme
- Courage to introduce and bring about cultural revolution
- Recognition and harnessing of gifts and talents in the nation
- Promoting team effort and discouraging unhealthy competition
- Redefining Excellence as ability to create opportunity for others
- Promoting a platform and incentive for Excellence
- Promoting international engagement, cooperation and under standing in sharing skills, expertise, and good practice
- Learning and skills revolution

In conclusion, no single person can bring about the change that is necessary to lead to progress in the Third World. It requires a team effort and holistic approach led by strong and visionary governments leading to the programme for change.

In a recent discussion with a leading coach from Europe who visited Africa he described it as a continent with some of the best talents in the world when it comes to football. However, he could not foresee Africa ever winning the World Cup as long as the players in their current form pursue their dream to score as individuals. According to this coach, the only way to win is to play as **a team and not as individuals**.

Unfortunately, what happens in football is a true reflection of African attitudes where people want to win and be recognised as individuals.

This scenario may be similar to watching a concert with every musician or singer wanting to be heard. Instead of sound and music, there is usually noise and distortion.

In our own department, lecturers share a common experience with our Third World students for their unwillingness and inability to work as a team. Invariably our Third World participants have no problem working with their Western counterparts and contributing their best. Yet when it comes to their fellow students from common background, there is usually the lack of trust, and a suspicion that others may steal their ideas.

On reflection, some of these students blame their lack of trust on their own educational experience of unhealthy competition through examinations aimed at failing and humiliating them even at their younger age. According to these students the experience has led to a culture of mistrust whereby learners seek to protect what they possess or have acquired and not give away, in order to ensure survival at competitive examinations and opportunities after college. As a result, their own education is seen as an arena of competition where individual interest and survival comes above society.

If these are the kind of citizens that the educational system is producing then, we have a big problem. Indeed, the kind that needs serious redress. It calls for a complete overhaul of the system in favour of that which tackles these cultural misconceptions and wins hearts and minds.

In the United Kingdom, it is estimated that less than five per cent of the population are the true wealth creators. They create jobs and opportunities for living for others. Indeed they create the platform for a 'Golden Economy'. This platform is supported by a workforce with the skills, attitudes and mindset that supports and sustains this 'Golden Economy.' In effect, those who create as well as those who labour to support and maintain this kind of wealth and opportunities will both have to acquire and maintain a 'Gold Mindset' as opposed to a 'coal mindset.'

Ironically, between 6 and 10 percent of this workforce are from Third World countries. They work extremely hard to impress their employers while in the UK. Yet when the same go back to their countries, most of these lay down their tools, expecting and waiting to be served or worshipped.

If Africa and the Third World are to revive their economies, there needs to be willingness to lay the foundations for creating opportunities for others. These nations just like Great Britain need 'Gold Minds', committed to the pursuit wealth and creation of opportunities for all, as well those committed to acquiring the knowledge, skills and attitudes necessary to sustain a growing economy. To come to this realisation, something needs to be done on the scale that will engage and transform the hearts and minds of all parties involved in the process of recovery. A truly Herculean task - but not impossible!

Beyond the Gold Mind
Education, Learning and Skills Revolution for the Twenty First Century

CHAPTER 11

11

In the United Kingdom, Great Britain and Western Europe is currently a new discovery which is carefully being pursued with the aim of sustaining a momentum of success in the face of competition with emerging economic superpowers such as India and China. In the United Kingdom this new philosophy has gained momentum as a result of recommendations from some leading wise men that led to an Act of Parliament and radical reforms in education and training.

An extract from white paper presented to parliament in 2007 reads as follows:

"It used to be that natural resources, a big labour force and a dose of inspiration was all that was required for countries to succeed, economically. But not any more. In the 21st century, our future prosperity will depend on building a
Britain where people are given the opportunity and encouragement to develop their skills and abilities to the maximum; and then given the support to rise as far as their talents will take them."

This extract is an indication of a new era and admission that the days where the nations success was inspired by few 'Gold Minds' are coming to an end as the world takes on new challenges.

This new discovery not only outlines the necessity for developing the

Third World countries to lay the foundation of nurturing 'Gold Minds'. There is the need to go even further in preparing the people to meet the challenges of the 21st century.

It seems to me that 'Gold Minds' still have significant roles to play in providing 'doses of inspiration' to these nations and their shattered economies. However that must only be seen as the starting point rather than an accomplishment.

In effect the realities and challenges of the 21st century which includes economic and energy crisis, global warming and environmental crisis, etc., are transforming the rules of engagement in a very dramatic way.

Once again the leadership of Great Britain in this area should give those that invariably subscribe to 'British education' an advantage in as much as they do not simply rely on 'British Colonial Education' in the 21st century.

My next volume 'Beyond the Gold Mind' explores innovation in education in Europe in general and the United Kingdom in particular and ways in which the rest of the world can benefit from these new ideas.

References

Binet. A, Wozniak. H R. Classics in Psychology, 1886: The Psychology of
Reasoning Vol 22 (History of Psychology) (Hardcover - 15 Oct 1998)

Bloom. B S., Krathwohl D. R., Masia. B. B., Taxonomy of Educational Objectives: Handbook 2 (Taxonomy of Educational Objectives)

Brenner .M, Pollack, R. Experimental Psychology of Alfred Binet
New York Springer Publishing 1969. Date Published: 1969

Burt, C.L., (1883–1971), psychometric psychologist and eugenicist

DfEE (1997) Excellence in schools. London: HMSO

DfEE (2001) Schools Building on success: raising standards, promoting diversity, achieving results. London: HMSO hhtp://www.dfee.gov.uk/buildingonsuccess/

DeBono, E. Lateral Thinking London: Penguin. (1970)

DeBono, E. Teach Your Child to Think London: Penguin. (1992)
Dickens, C. Hard Times: For These Times, 1854

Feuerstein, R. Rand, Y., Hoffman, M.B. and Miller, R. Instrumental Enrichment: an intervention programme for cognitive modifiability Baltimore: University Park Press. (1980)

Fisher, P. (Editor) Thinking Through History Cambridge: Chris Kington Publishing. (2001)

DfEE [Web Archives] **History of thinking skills in the UK**
Gillborn and Gipps (1996): Recent Research on the Achievements of Ethnic minority pupils(Gilborn and Gipps1996, p.82)

Gillborn, D. & Mirza, HEdcuational Inequality: mapping race, calss and gender London: OFSTED . (2000)

Green paper 1997: Excellent for all children- Meeting special Educational Needs
(DfEE1997, p.3)

Jackson. J Snr. TV Broadcast Chicago August 2007

Milman, W H, `The Education of the People` published in the Quartely Review (vol 78 -1846)
Moon, B. & Shelton Mayes, A. Teaching and Learning in the secondary school. London: Routledge/ou (1994)

Moyles, J. Beginnin Teaching, Beginning Learning. Oxford:OUP. (1995)

OFSTED (1999) Raising the Attainment of minority Ethnic pupils: Schools and LEA Responses

Pollard, A. & Bourne, J. (eds.) Teaching and Learning in the primary school. London Rutledge/OU. (1994)

QCA DfEE (1995) English in the National Curriculum. London: HMSO

QCA DfEE (1999) The National Curriculum: Handbook for primary teachers in England London:

SCAA (1996) A guide to the National Curriculum. London: HMSO.
SCAA (1994) The National Curriculum and its Assessment: Final Report (Dearing report). London: SCAA

Teachers and Teaching, Volume 4, Issue 2 October 1998, pages 317 – 330 Rout ledge

About the Author

Obeng De Lawrence is a Medical Scientist and, Lecturer by profession, and Educationalist in the UK. He is a Minister of religion and a motivational speaker. Obeng De Lawrence is also the Principal and Founder of International Teachers College [ITC] –London and Director of Choice UK.

Other Titles by the Author

Beyond the Gold Mind

In this book, I introduce the reader to a learning revolution currently adopted by Europe and the United Kingdom in their bid to lead the way in overcoming the challenges of twenty first century. The reader will discover a thrilling revelation as to why leading thinkers in the United Kingdom believe that the kind of education that sustained the empire until the end of the twentieth century has had its day. This volume is put together to enable the reader to become familiar with some aspects of lifelong learning in the UK

The Dream Harvest

In this book, I have made an attempt to inspire readers to nurture their dreams to success. I have also explained the real purposes for living and how to aspire to great success. This work is designed to assist the reader to discover simple and practical steps about making his or her dream happen.

"If you can identify your 'Dream' and all the things needed to make it happen, you would have discovered your God-given potential – Your Dream Harvest!"

It is possible that after reading this book, you will be able to say:

"Yes, I can"

The Ideal Learner

In this book I have discussed ways in which learning can be effective in the 21st century and make the learner successful and functional within society. The author discusses the best approaches to learning, and ways to be successful not only in the classroom but also at work and within society. This is packaged for all learner and teachers both young and adult, and whether at school, college, university, work, home or in the community.

The Ideal Teacher

In this book the author discussed ways in which teaching can be effective in the 21st century and make the learner successful and functional within society. The author discusses the best approaches to teaching, and ways to be successful not only in the classroom but also at work and within society. The author aims at enabling and assisting teachers to adapt to modern methods of teaching and meet international standards under the concepts and philosophies of lifelong learning.

7

www.ingramcontent.com/pod-product-compliance
Lightning Source LLC
Chambersburg PA
CBHW021834300426
44114CB00009BA/443